I0011639

Table of Contents

Chapter 1 – Introduction

The Model-View-ViewModel design pattern is a hot topic in the WPF and Silverlight community these days. There is a lot of great information available on the Web to help people learn the basics of the pattern, but eventually the free ride comes to an end. There are some common design problems inherent in most MVVM applications whose solutions are neither well known nor documented. This e-book exists to help fill that gap.

By the time you have finished reading this e-book, you will have learned best practices for overcoming those common hurdles. I have successfully used all of the techniques presented here in production applications, and know from experience what works and what does not. In addition to tackling some specific MVVM design problems, we will also review the high-level architecture of a WPF/MVVM application and discuss the decisions that went into creating it.

More specifically, we will review the following topics:

- Best practices for designing Views

- Best practices for designing ViewModels

- Deciding on what state and logic belongs in Views versus ViewModels

- Coordinating animated transitions between the ViewModel and View

- Implementing unlimited undo functionality that involves animated transitions

- Working with modal dialogs from the ViewModel layer

The Demo Application

The topics covered in this e-book are explained in the context of a WPF game that I created, called BubbleBurst. It is a variation of a popular game called BubbleBreaker, which is widely available on mobile phones and the Web. I must warn you that this game is highly addictive, and should not be played for prolonged periods of time!

A screenshot of the game in action can be seen below:

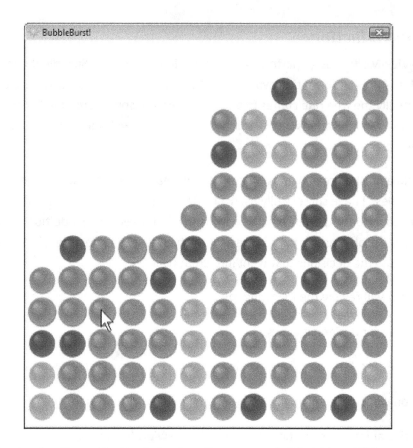

The game is quite simple. Your objective is to clear the screen of all bubbles. Click on a group of bubbles to remove them from the screen. Two adjacent bubbles are part of a group if one bubble is directly above, below, to the right, or to the left of another bubble of the same color. After you burst a group of bubbles, the bubbles above the group will fall down to fill the empty spaces left behind. Then all bubbles to the left of newly vacated spaces will move as far right as possible to occupy those empty spaces. Once there are no more bubble groups left the game is over.

When the game ends, you are shown the game-over dialog, as seen below:

Additionally, the window's right-click context menu gives you two options. You can use it to restart the game, and to un-burst bubble groups, in case you make a mistake. If you prefer, you can press Ctrl + Z to perform an undo.

The Source Code

The BubbleBurst source code is hosted on the CodePlex website. In addition to downloading the source code, you can also make use of the CodePlex project to ask and answer questions about this e-book, report bugs, and get the latest updates.

Please visit the CodePlex project here: http://bubbleburst.codeplex.com

BubbleBurst was created in Visual Studio 2008 with Service Pack 1. It compiles against .NET 3.5 with Service Pack 1. The code was written in C#, making heavy use of LINQ and many of the language enhancements introduced in C# 3.0. The system requirements for running the application are the standard requirements for any WPF application. There are no special dependencies that must be installed in order for the game to run.

Chapter 2 – Brief Overview of WPF and MVVM

This chapter is intended to help someone who is fairly new to WPF and/or MVVM get an idea of the big picture. It might also be interesting for a seasoned veteran looking to get a different perspective on familiar topics. All subsequent chapters are for people who are already up-to-speed with WPF and MVVM. If you don't want or need to read this chapter, feel free to skip ahead to the next chapter now.

WPF

Microsoft's Windows Presentation Foundation (WPF) is a user interface programming platform that operates on top of the .NET Framework. It has a mile long feature list, so we won't cover everything it can do. Instead, let's focus on the things that are most important for understanding how BubbleBurst works.

The most salient feature of the platform to know about while reading this book is its data binding system. I have met quite a few developers who switched from Windows Forms to WPF just because of its incredible data binding capabilities. Data binding is an automated way to move data objects from one place to another. You can specify when, how, and why a binding will transfer values between its source and target. It's possible to bind a property on one UI element to a property on another UI element, or even to bind an element to itself. Additionally, value converters make it possible to bind two properties of different types. Bindings can be created in code or markup.

User interfaces in WPF are typically declared in a markup language known as XAML, which stands for eXtensible Application Markup Language. It is an XML-based format useful for declaring a graph of .NET objects, and configuring those objects with property values and event handling methods. XAML files are often associated with a code-behind file, which allows you to have code, such as event handling methods, which responds to events of the controls declared in XAML. A XAML file and its code-behind both contain partials of the same class, which means that you can access from code the objects declared in XAML, and vice versa.

Several controls, such as Button and MenuItem, allow you to bypass the code-behind altogether via their Command property. If you set a button's Command property to an object that implements the ICommand interface, when the user clicks the button it will automatically execute the command. As we will see soon, declaring a binding to a command in XAML can help simplify your application's design.

Arranging UI elements into various layouts is the bread and butter of user interface development. In WPF you can achieve an endless variety of layouts by leveraging its support for panels. The term 'panel' refers to an element container that knows where to place its child elements relative to each other, based on their size and the layout logic coded into the panel. Some panels will resize their child elements in order to achieve the desired layout. WPF includes the abstract Panel class, from which the common panels, such as Grid and StackPanel, derive. If you need to use coordinate-based positioning (i.e. use X and Y offsets), the Canvas panel allows you to gain that level of layout precision.

All but the simplest of demo applications must display a list of objects. WPF treats a list of objects as a first-class citizen by providing you with ItemsControl. Many common controls derive from ItemsControl, such as ListBox and ListView. Its ItemsSource property can be set to any collection of objects. ItemsControl generates UI elements that render those objects. You can tell the ItemsControl what UI elements to render each item with by setting the ItemTemplate property to a custom DataTemplate. In complex scenarios, you can use an ItemTemplateSelector to programmatically select a DataTemplate based on values of the data object. Another great feature of ItemsControl is that it allows you to specify the layout panel with which it arranges its child elements. You can use any layout panel, including a custom panel, as the ItemsPanel to achieve your desired layout strategy for the ItemsControl's child elements.

One other thing to know about about WPF that will help BubbleBurst make sense is that it uses a "retained" rendering system. Unlike Windows Forms, and other HWND-based UI platforms, in WPF you very rarely ever need to write code that paints the screen. As opposed to a "destructive" rendering system, WPF's retained rendering system caches vector drawing instructions and intelligently manages the job of handling things like region invalidations for you. You provide WPF with a description of what you want rendered, via high-level objects like Ellipse and TextBlock, and it works out what needs to be drawn to the screen when and where.

Learn More about WPF

If you would like to learn more about WPF before reading further, consider visiting these links:

Introduction to Windows Presentation Foundation

http://msdn.microsoft.com/en-us/library/aa970268.aspx

WPF Architecture

http://msdn.microsoft.com/en-us/library/ms750441.aspx

A Guided Tour of WPF

http://joshsmithonwpf.wordpress.com/a-guided-tour-of-wpf/

Customize Data Display with Data Binding and WPF

http://msdn.microsoft.com/en-us/magazine/cc700358.aspx

ItemsControl: 'I' is for Item Container via Dr. WPF

http://drwpf.com/blog/2008/03/25/itemscontrol-i-is-for-item-container/

MVVM

It was once commonly said that all roads lead to Rome. Today, all WPF and Silverlight best practices lead to the Model-View-ViewModel design pattern. MVVM has become a common way of discussing, designing, and implementing WPF and Silverlight programs. Like all other design patterns, it is a set of practical guidelines and ideas that can help you create structurally sound software that is maintainable and understandable. Like all other design patterns, it provides you with a common vocabulary with which you can have meaningful discussions with your technical colleagues. It takes root in the Model-View-Presenter design pattern, but diverges in ways that enable you to leverage capabilities of the UI platform to simplify your life as a developer.

MVVM implies three broad categories of objects. Model objects contain the data consumed and modified by the user. They can also include things like business rule processing, input validation, change tracking, and other things related to your system's data. Views, on the other hand, are entirely visual. A View is a UI control that displays data, allows the user to modify the state of the program via device input (i.e. keyboard and mouse), shows videos, displays a photo album, or whatever else your users want to see on the screen. So far, so good. Now let's talk about the middleman: the ViewModel.

A ViewModel is a model of a view.

In case that sentence didn't clarify the topic enough, let's dig a little deeper. First of all, a ViewModel is not merely the new code-behind for a View. That is a common misconception, which totally misses the point. If someone considers ViewModels to be a new form of code-behind, then they probably have too much of their program written in code-behind files. When using ViewModels, your Views can and, in many cases, *should* still have certain kinds of code in their code-behind files. The ViewModel is an abstraction of the user interface. It should have no knowledge of the UI elements on the screen. Logic that deals specifically with objects scoped to a particular View should exist in that View's code-behind.

"What is the point of having ViewModels?" you might be wondering. There are several reasons to create and use ViewModels. The most important reason is that it allows you to treat the user interface of an application as a logical system that can be designed with the same quality of engineering and object orientation that you apply to other parts of your application. This includes the ability to easily write unit and integration tests for the functionality of the user interface, without having to get into the messy world of writing tests for live UIs. It means that the Views that render your ViewModels can be modified or replaced whenever necessary, and little to no changes should be required in the ViewModel classes. It also means that you can use frameworks like MEF to dynamically compose your ViewModels, to easily support plug-in architectures in the user interface layer.

The fundamental mechanisms involved in creating applications based on MVVM are data binding and commands. ViewModel objects expose properties to which Views are bound, including properties that return command objects. When the properties of a ViewModel change, the Views bound to that ViewModel receive a notification when the ViewModel raises its PropertyChanged event (which is the sole member of the INotifyPropertyChanged interface). The data binding system will automatically get the new value from the modified property and update the bound properties in the View. Similarly, changes made to the data in the View are pushed back to the ViewModel via bindings. When the user clicks on a button whose Command property is bound to a command exposed by a ViewModel, that command executes and allows the ViewModel to act on the user's interaction. If the ViewModel needs to expose a modifiable collection of objects to a View, the ViewModel can use ObservableCollection<T> to get collection change notifications for free (which the binding system knows how to work with). It's all very simple to implement because data bindings do the grunt work of moving bound data values around when necessary.

The magic glue that ties Views and ViewModels together is, more often than not, the DataContext property inherited by all visual elements. When a View is created, its DataContext can be set to a ViewModel so that all elements in the View can easily bind to it. This is not a hard and fast rule, though. Some people prefer to put their ViewModels into resource dictionaries and bind to them via resource references. That technique can make it easier to work with Views in Microsoft's Expression Blend visual design tool.

Learn More about MVVM

If you would like to learn more about MVVM before reading further, consider visiting these links:

WPF Apps with the Model-View-ViewModel Design Pattern

http://msdn.microsoft.com/en-us/magazine/dd419663.aspx

Simplifying the WPF TreeView by Using the ViewModel Pattern

http://www.codeproject.com/KB/WPF/TreeViewWithViewModel.aspx

Hands-On Model-View-ViewModel (MVVM) for Silverlight and WPF

http://weblogs.asp.net/craigshoemaker/archive/2009/02/26/hands-on-model-view-viewmodel-mvvm-for-silverlight-and-wpf.aspx

M-V-VM via Karl Shifflett

http://karlshifflett.wordpress.com/mvvm/

MVVM Light Toolkit via Laurent Bugnion

http://www.galasoft.ch/mvvm/getstarted/

MVVM Foundation via Josh Smith

http://mvvmfoundation.codeplex.com/

Chapter 3 – View Architecture Overview

The next two chapters are an overview of BubbleBurst's View and ViewModel layers. We will explore the high-level structure of these two layers of the application. Subsequent chapters dive deeper into how the application solves specific problems that are common in MVVM applications. Let's begin by examining how the various Views work together to create the BubbleBurst user interface.

The BubbleBurst Visual Studio solution contains three projects. The project that builds the executable is called *BubbleBurst*. It only contains the XAML needed to configure an Application object and a Window. All game-specific UI controls exist in the *BubbleBurst.View* project, which is referenced by the *BubbleBurst* project.

As you can see in the following screenshot from the Mole visualizer [http://moleproject.com/], the game's visual tree is not very complicated:

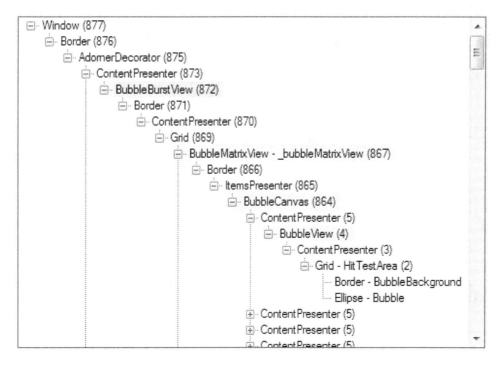

The highlighted nodes represent the Views and custom panel reviewed in the remainder of this chapter.

BubbleBurstView

The top-level View is called BubbleBurstView. It is the content of the application's main window. It hosts three things: the matrix of bubbles, the game-over dialog, and a context menu. Since it is only a container for other major views, it does not have many responsibilities aside from starting a new game once the UI is loaded, and processing keystrokes. The application's top-level ViewModel object is created in this View, as we will see in the next chapter.

The following XAML shows the BubbleBurstView control with all of the irrelevant details removed, for the sake of clarity:

```
<UserControl xmlns:view="clr-namespace:BubbleBurst.View">
  <UserControl.ContextMenu>
    <ContextMenu>
      <MenuItem Header="Undo" />
      <MenuItem Header="Restart" />
    </ContextMenu>
  </UserControl.ContextMenu>
  <Grid>
    <view:BubbleMatrixView />
    <view:GameOverView />
  </Grid>
</UserControl>
```

BubbleMatrixView

BubbleMatrixView is the UI control responsible for displaying bubbles in a fixed-size grid arrangement. It is an ItemsControl subclass that makes use of the ItemTemplate and ItemsPanel properties to create a databound matrix of bubbles that burst and slide around. Isn't WPF amazing?!

Here is the markup that configures BubbleMatrixView:

```
<ItemsControl
  x:Class="BubbleBurst.View.BubbleMatrixView"
  xmlns="http://schemas.microsoft.com/winfx/2006/xaml/presentation"
  xmlns:x="http://schemas.microsoft.com/winfx/2006/xaml"
  xmlns:view="clr-namespace:BubbleBurst.View"
  Background="White"
  IsEnabled="{Binding Path=IsIdle}"
  ItemsSource="{Binding Path=Bubbles, Mode=OneTime}"
  >
  <!-- All bubbles live in a BubbleCanvas panel. -->
  <ItemsControl.ItemsPanel>
    <ItemsPanelTemplate>
      <view:BubbleCanvas Loaded="HandleBubbleCanvasLoaded" />
    </ItemsPanelTemplate>
  </ItemsControl.ItemsPanel>

  <!-- Render each BubbleViewModel with a BubbleView control. -->
  <ItemsControl.ItemTemplate>
    <DataTemplate>
      <view:BubbleView />
    </DataTemplate>
  </ItemsControl.ItemTemplate>
</ItemsControl>
```

The BubbleMatrixView code-behind contains an event handling method for the Loaded event of its ItemsPanel. We review that panel in the next section, but for now let's check out what this control does when its ItemsPanel loads:

```csharp
void HandleBubbleCanvasLoaded(object sender, RoutedEventArgs e)
{
    // Store a reference to the panel that contains the bubbles.
    _bubbleCanvas = sender as BubbleCanvas;

    // Create the factory that makes Storyboards
    // used after a bubble group bursts.
    _storyboardFactory = new BubblesTaskStoryboardFactory(_bubbleCanvas);

    // Let the world know that the size of the bubble matrix is known.
    this.RaiseMatrixDimensionsAvailable();
}

void RaiseMatrixDimensionsAvailable()
{
    var handler = this.MatrixDimensionsAvailable;
    if (handler != null)
    {
        handler(this, EventArgs.Empty);
    }
}

/// <summary>
/// Raised when the RowCount and ColumnCount
/// properties have meaningful values.
/// </summary>
internal event EventHandler MatrixDimensionsAvailable;

/// <summary>
/// Returns the number of columns in the bubble matrix.
/// </summary>
internal int ColumnCount
{
    get { return _bubbleCanvas != null ? _bubbleCanvas.ColumnCount : -1; }
}

/// <summary>
/// Returns the number of rows in the bubble matrix.
/// </summary>
internal int RowCount
{
    get { return _bubbleCanvas != null ? _bubbleCanvas.RowCount : -1; }
}
```

There are some other interesting things going on in BubbleMatrixView's code-behind file, which we will review in depth in Chapter 5. For now, let's see how the ItemsPanel works…

BubbleCanvas

The ItemsPanel used by BubbleMatrixView is a custom panel I wrote called BubbleCanvas. It derives from WPF's Canvas panel and introduces some functionality useful for managing the location of bubbles it contains. One of its key features is that it sets the initial location of each bubble. The panel uses some information about the logical location of a bubble from the child element's ViewModel (discussed in the next chapter) in order to calculate the proper location for that element. That code is seen below:

```
protected override void OnVisualChildrenChanged(
    DependencyObject visualAdded,
    DependencyObject visualRemoved)
{
    var contentPresenter = visualAdded as ContentPresenter;
    if (contentPresenter != null)
    {
        var bubble = contentPresenter.DataContext as BubbleViewModel;
        if (bubble != null)
        {
            Canvas.SetLeft(contentPresenter, CalculateLeft(bubble.Column));
            Canvas.SetTop(contentPresenter, CalculateTop(bubble.Row));

            contentPresenter.Width = BubbleSize;
            contentPresenter.Height = BubbleSize;
        }
    }
    base.OnVisualChildrenChanged(visualAdded, visualRemoved);
}

double CalculateLeft(int column)
{
    double bubblesWidth = BubbleSize * this.ColumnCount;
    double horizOffset = (base.ActualWidth - bubblesWidth) / 2;
    return column * BubbleSize + horizOffset;
}

double CalculateTop(int row)
{
    double bubblesHeight = BubbleSize * this.RowCount;
    double vertOffset = (base.ActualHeight - bubblesHeight) / 2;
    return row * BubbleSize + vertOffset;
}
```

As previously seen in the screenshot of this application's visual tree, each BubbleView instance is the child element of a ContentPresenter. Those ContentPresenters are the child elements of BubbleCanvas, which is why the panel adjusts the location and size of them instead of the BubbleViews. Once those initial element locations are established BubbleCanvas will never adjust them again. All subsequent bubble movements are performed elsewhere, which is the topic of Chapter 5.

BubbleView

Each bubble displayed in the bubble matrix is an instance of BubbleView. That control is a Button subclass that contains three elements. It uses a Grid panel to capture mouse clicks, an Ellipse element to render a circular bubble, and a Border that provides a subtle drop shadow when a bubble is in the highlighted bubble group. The complete markup from the BubbleView.xaml file is seen below:

```xml
<Button
  x:Class="BubbleBurst.View.BubbleView"
  xmlns="http://schemas.microsoft.com/winfx/2006/xaml/presentation"
  xmlns:x="http://schemas.microsoft.com/winfx/2006/xaml"
  Command="{Binding Path=BurstBubbleGroupCommand}"
  RenderTransformOrigin="0.5,0.5"
  Template="{DynamicResource BubbleTemplate}"
  >
  <Button.Triggers>
    <!-- This causes the bubble to animate into view. -->
    <EventTrigger RoutedEvent="Button.Loaded">
      <BeginStoryboard
        Storyboard="{DynamicResource BubbleLoadedStoryboard}"
        />
    </EventTrigger>
  </Button.Triggers>

  <!-- These transforms are used during animations. -->
  <Button.RenderTransform>
    <TransformGroup>
      <ScaleTransform />
      <TranslateTransform />
    </TransformGroup>
  </Button.RenderTransform>

  <!-- The Grid captures mouse clicks. -->
  <Grid
    x:Name="HitTestArea"
    x:FieldModifier="private"
    Background="Transparent"
    IsHitTestVisible="True"
    Style="{StaticResource BubbleGridStyle}"
    >
    <!-- The Border provides a dark rim when in a bubble group. -->
    <Border
      x:Name="BubbleBackground"
      x:FieldModifier="private"
      IsHitTestVisible="False"
      Style="{StaticResource BubbleBackgroundBorderStyle}"
      />
    <!-- The Ellipse draws a bubble. -->
    <Ellipse
      x:Name="Bubble"
      x:FieldModifier="private"
      IsHitTestVisible="False"
      Style="{DynamicResource BubbleEllipseStyle}"
      />
  </Grid>
</Button>
```

Note that the Button's Command property is bound the BurstBubbleGroupCommand property on the ViewModel. That will come into play later on, when we examine BubbleViewModel.

There is a separate file called BubbleViewResources.xaml that contains a ResourceDictionary full of resources used to render and animate a BubbleView. One of the resources it contains is the Style applied to the Ellipse element used to render a circular bubble. That Style contains DataTriggers which determine the brush used to paint a bubble the appropriate color.

Here is the markup for that Style:

```xml
<Style x:Key="BubbleEllipseStyle" TargetType="{x:Type Ellipse}">
  <Setter Property="Margin" Value="3" />
  <Style.Triggers>
    <DataTrigger Binding="{Binding Path=BubbleType}" Value="RedBubble">
      <Setter Property="Fill" Value="{StaticResource RedBubbleBrush}" />
    </DataTrigger>
    <DataTrigger Binding="{Binding Path=BubbleType}" Value="GreenBubble">
      <Setter Property="Fill" Value="{StaticResource GreenBubbleBrush}" />
    </DataTrigger>
    <DataTrigger Binding="{Binding Path=BubbleType}" Value="BlueBubble">
      <Setter Property="Fill" Value="{StaticResource BlueBubbleBrush}" />
    </DataTrigger>
    <DataTrigger Binding="{Binding Path=BubbleType}" Value="OrangeBubble">
      <Setter Property="Fill" Value="{StaticResource OrangeBubbleBrush}" />
    </DataTrigger>
    <DataTrigger Binding="{Binding Path=BubbleType}" Value="PurpleBubble">
      <Setter Property="Fill" Value="{StaticResource PurpleBubbleBrush}" />
    </DataTrigger>
  </Style.Triggers>
</Style>
```

GameOverView

Once the game has ended, the user is shown the GameOverView. It behaves like a modal dialog box, forcing the user to select an option before it is dismissed. GameOverView displays information about the outcome of the game, and allows the user to either play again or close the application. When the game ends this dialog bounces onto the screen, and flies away when the user clicks 'PLAY AGAIN'.

We will closely examine how this View works in Chapter 7.

What Should a View Do?

In Chapter 2 I touched on the hotly debated topic of what belongs in a View's code-behind. Some people believe that it's not a problem to put as much code as you want into the code-behind, claiming that it simplifies development and, thus, increases productivity. Unless they are working on extremely simple user interfaces all the time, they are misguided.

Others insist that there should never be a single line of code in the code-behind, based on the strange notion that **code** does not belong in the **code**-behind. What an odd bunch! In all seriousness, the arguments in favor of having nothing in the code-behind usually stem from testability concerns. Unit and integration testing advocates try to externalize as much code from a View as possible, because live UI objects are notoriously difficult to programmatically test. While there is merit in this argument, anything taken to extremes becomes disadvantageous in the long run. Unless they are willing and able to maintain unnecessary layers of abstraction and indirection just for the sake of testing every last line of code in their applications, they, too, are misguided.

Practical developers take the middle road and use good judgment to determine what code belongs where, as opposed to blindly adhering to a dysfunctional dogma. Throughout the BubbleBurst source code you can find examples of code-behind files that contain logic specific to the functioning of a View. In non-trivial user interfaces there are various bits of code required to make a View work properly. If that code relies on UI elements, resources, or anything else belonging to the realm of the user interface, I see no reason not to put that code into the View's code-behind. The one exception to this rule is that you can, for certain types of problems, encapsulate reusable View functionality into attached behaviors. Nothing is ever simple!

Chapter 4 – ViewModel Architecture Overview

Each of the Views examined in the previous chapter has a corresponding ViewModel class. The ViewModel classes can be found in the *BubbleBurst.ViewModel* project, which is referenced by the *BubbleBurst.View* project. Each View's DataContext is set to its ViewModel object, which makes it easy to data bind to the ViewModel in XAML. The following class diagram shows how the major ViewModel objects relate to each other:

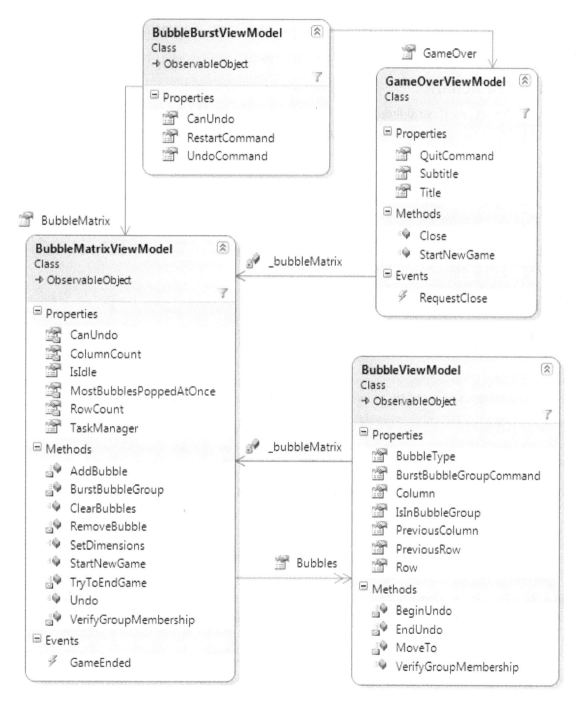

Now that we have a broad understanding of the ViewModels, we can examine them in more detail.

Core ViewModel Classes

BubbleBurst's ViewModel project references my MVVM Foundation library on CodePlex. It contains several useful classes for developers writing ViewModels. The MVVM Foundation classes used in this application are ObservableObject and RelayCommand. ObservableObject is the base class for any type that must support property change notifications for data binding purposes (i.e. classes that implement INotifyPropertyChanged). All command objects created by ViewModels are instances of RelayCommand. That class allows you to inject execution logic into a command by passing delegates to its constructor. It eliminates the need to create a class that implements ICommand for each command exposed by ViewModel objects.

BubbleBurstViewModel

Just as how BubbleBurstView is considered to be the top-level View, BubbleBurstViewModel is the top-level ViewModel. An instance of BubbleBurstViewModel is declared as the DataContext of BubbleBurstView in its XAML file. That declaration is seen below:

```
<UserControl.DataContext>
  <viewModel:BubbleBurstViewModel />
</UserControl.DataContext>
```

The constructor of BubbleBurstViewModel creates a BubbleMatrixViewModel and hooks its GameEnded event in order to create a GameOverViewModel.

```
public BubbleBurstViewModel()
{
    this.BubbleMatrix = new BubbleMatrixViewModel();
    this.BubbleMatrix.GameEnded += delegate
    {
        this.GameOver = new GameOverViewModel(this.BubbleMatrix);
        this.GameOver.RequestClose += this.HandleGameOverRequestClose;
    };
}

void HandleGameOverRequestClose(object sender, EventArgs e)
{
    this.GameOver.RequestClose -= this.HandleGameOverRequestClose;
    this.GameOver = null;
}
```

This class does not do much besides create its child ViewModel objects, respond to events, and expose commands that delegate work. Those commands are bound to by menu items in the context menu declared in BubbleBurstView. One example of this command-driven delegation technique can be found in the RestartCommand property. When the user clicks the 'Restart' context menu item, it results in the execution of this command:

```
public ICommand RestartCommand
{
    get { return new RelayCommand(this.BubbleMatrix.StartNewGame); }
}
```

The context menu item whose Command property is bound to RestartCommand is in BubbleBurstView.

```
<MenuItem Header="Restart" Command="{Binding Path=RestartCommand}" />
```

It might seem as though placing the RestartCommand property on BubbleBurstViewModel and having the command delegate to BubbleMatrixViewModel is unnecessary. Why not just expose the command on BubbleMatrixViewModel? I chose to do it this way because the UndoCommand property creates a command whose can-execute logic depends on the state of the BubbleBurstViewModel instance. Since that command must exist in BubbleBurstViewModel, the ContextMenu must be in BubbleBurstView. It makes sense to keep all command properties used by the same context menu at the same level of the ViewModel hierarchy, for the sake of simplicity.

There is no need for the RestartCommand property to store a backing field reference to the RelayCommand instance it creates. This is because the MenuItem's Command property binding will only pull a value from RestartCommand the first time the user opens the menu. The parameter passed into the RelayCommand constructor points to a method on the BubbleMatrixViewModel object owned by BubbleBurstViewModel. That method is invoked when the command is executed in response to a click on the 'Restart' menu item.

As we saw earlier, BubbleBurstViewModel's constructor creates an instance of BubbleMatrixViewModel and assigns it to the BubbleMatrix property. That object is the brains of this whole operation, so let's check it out next.

BubbleMatrixViewModel

The fixed-size grid of bubbles seen in the UI is rendered by BubbleMatrixView. That class, which we examined in the previous chapter, is responsible for displaying an instance of BubbleMatrixViewModel. The bubble matrix makes use of several other classes in the ViewModel project to get its job done. Throughout the next few chapters we will see how those various objects cooperate to provide the user with a fun game to play. In this section we narrow in on a specific subset of the bubble matrix functionality. Let's begin by looking over the following class diagram, which shows the relevant classes and some of their members:

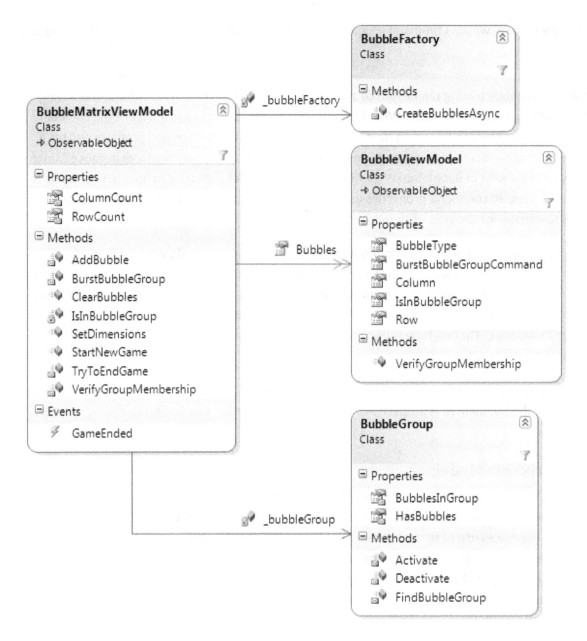

Creating Bubbles with BubbleFactory

Now it's time to see how bubbles are created and added to the bubble matrix. As you might have guessed, the BubbleFactory class is responsible for creating instances of BubbleViewModel and adding them to the bubble matrix's Bubbles collection. That class exposes a CreateBubblesAsync method which causes the bubbles to be created over time. BubbleMatrixViewModel invokes that method when a new game starts, as seen below:

```
public void StartNewGame()
{
    // Reset game state.
    this.IsIdle = true;
    _bubbleGroup.BubblesInGroup.Clear();
    _bubbleGroupSizeStack.Clear();
```

```
    this.TaskManager.Reset();

    // Create a new matrix of bubbles.
    this.ClearBubbles();
    _bubbleFactory.CreateBubblesAsync();
}
```

The reason why bubbles are created asynchronously has to do with user experience requirements. I wanted the bubbles to appear and animate into place at random, because it adds an element of fun and visual interest. The following code shows how BubbleFactory works:

```
/// <summary>
/// Populates the bubble matrix with new bubbles over time.
/// </summary>
internal void CreateBubblesAsync()
{
    _timer.Stop();

    _bubbleStagingArea.Clear();
    _bubbleStagingArea.AddRange(
        from row in Enumerable.Range(0, _bubbleMatrix.RowCount)
        from col in Enumerable.Range(0, _bubbleMatrix.ColumnCount)
        select new BubbleViewModel(_bubbleMatrix, row, col));

    _bubbleMatrix.IsIdle = false;

    _timer.Start();
}

void HandleTimerTick(object sender, EventArgs e)
{
    if (!_timer.IsEnabled)
        return;

    for (int i = 0; i < 4 && _bubbleStagingArea.Any(); ++i)
    {
        // Get a random bubble from the staging area.
        int index = _random.Next(0, _bubbleStagingArea.Count);
        var bubble = _bubbleStagingArea[index];
        _bubbleStagingArea.RemoveAt(index);

        // Add the bubble to the bubble matrix.
        _bubbleMatrix.AddBubble(bubble);

        if (!_bubbleStagingArea.Any())
        {
            _timer.Stop();
            _bubbleMatrix.IsIdle = true;
        }
    }
}
```

The _timer field is an instance of DispatcherTimer. I used that type of timer to stagger the creation of bubbles because it ensures that the method which handles its Tick event is invoked on the UI thread.

Since the bubbles are being added to an ObservableCollection, and WPF requires collection change notifications to occur on the UI thread, this prevents cross-thread violations.

All of the BubbleViewModel objects are created up front and added to a "staging area" list, in the CreateBubblesAsync method. When the timer ticks, several bubbles are removed from the staging area at random and added to the bubble matrix. They immediately appear on-screen in the BubbleMatrixView after being added to the Bubbles collection, because it is an ObservableCollection<BubbleViewModel>.

BubbleFactory sets the bubble matrix's IsIdle property to false before starting to add bubbles to the user interface. After the last bubble is added, it sets that property back to true. BubbleMatrixView has its IsEnabled property bound to the IsIdle property. This ensures that while bubbles are being added to the matrix the user cannot burst bubble groups. The IsIdle property is also set to false during the animated transitions after the user bursts, or un-bursts, a bubble group. Before we see how those animated transitions work, we need to see how bubble groups are found in the first place.

Finding Bubble Groups

The user can burst groups of bubbles that are the same color and adjacent to one another. When the user moves the mouse cursor over a group of bubbles, each bubble in the group expands a little bit and has a subtle drop shadow. The expansion and deflation is animated, which provides a gentle visual cue.

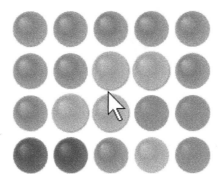

Supporting this functionality requires the ViewModel layer to know how to determine if the bubble under the mouse cursor is part of a bubble group. It also needs to inform each bubble in a group that it is, in fact, in a group. The following code, from BubbleView.xaml.cs, starts the bubble group processing:

```
BubbleViewModel _bubble;

void HandleDataContextChanged(object sender, DependencyPropertyChangedEventArgs e)
{
    _bubble = e.NewValue as BubbleViewModel;
}

void HandleMouseEnter(object sender, MouseEventArgs e)
{
    if (_bubble != null)
        _bubble.VerifyGroupMembership(true);
}
```

```
void HandleMouseLeave(object sender, MouseEventArgs e)
{
    if (_bubble != null)
        _bubble.VerifyGroupMembership(false);
}
```

When the mouse cursor enters a BubbleView control a call is made to BubbleViewModel's VerifyGroupMembership method. The end result of that method call is a potential change made to the BubbleViewModel's IsInBubbleGroup property. Here is the method in BubbleViewModel that gets invoked:

```
/// <summary>
/// Causes the bubble to evaluate whether or not it is in a bubble group.
/// </summary>
/// <param name="isMouseOver">
/// True if the mouse cursor is currently over this bubble.
/// </param>
public void VerifyGroupMembership(bool isMouseOver)
{
    _bubbleMatrix.VerifyGroupMembership(isMouseOver ? this : null);
}
```

As you can see above, this method is just a pass-through to the VerifyGroupMembership method of BubbleMatrixViewModel. This layer of indirection is justified by the fact that a BubbleView should not know anything about the existence of a bubble matrix, and an individual BubbleViewModel does not have enough information to satisfy the request of verifying its group membership. The real logic for processing this request is further up the ViewModel hierarchy. Here is the method in BubbleMatrixViewModel that gets invoked:

```
internal void VerifyGroupMembership(BubbleViewModel bubble)
{
    _bubbleGroup.Deactivate();
    if (bubble != null)
        _bubbleGroup.FindBubbleGroup(bubble).Activate();
}
```

BubbleMatrixViewModel delegates this work to an instance of the BubbleGroup class. That class is responsible for locating a bubble group, storing the bubbles in the most recently located group, and informing each bubble that it is in a group.

The logic that actually finds a bubble group in the BubbleGroup class is shown below:

```
internal BubbleGroup FindBubbleGroup(BubbleViewModel bubble)
{
    if (bubble == null)
        throw new ArgumentNullException("bubble");

    bool isBubbleInCurrentGroup = this.BubblesInGroup.Contains(bubble);
    if (!isBubbleInCurrentGroup)
    {
        this.BubblesInGroup.Clear();
```

```csharp
            this.SearchForGroup(bubble);

            bool addOriginalBubble =
                this.HasBubbles &&
                !this.BubblesInGroup.Contains(bubble);

            if (addOriginalBubble)
            {
                this.BubblesInGroup.Add(bubble);
            }
        }

        return this;
    }

    void SearchForGroup(BubbleViewModel bubble)
    {
        foreach (BubbleViewModel groupMember in this.FindMatchingNeighbors(bubble))
        {
            if (!this.BubblesInGroup.Contains(groupMember))
            {
                this.BubblesInGroup.Add(groupMember);
                this.SearchForGroup(groupMember);
            }
        }
    }

    IEnumerable<BubbleViewModel> FindMatchingNeighbors(BubbleViewModel bubble)
    {
        var matches = new List<BubbleViewModel>();

        // Check above.
        var match = this.TryFindMatch(bubble.Row - 1, bubble.Column, bubble.BubbleType);
        if (match != null)
            matches.Add(match);

        // Check below.
        match = this.TryFindMatch(bubble.Row + 1, bubble.Column, bubble.BubbleType);
        if (match != null)
            matches.Add(match);

        // Check left.
        match = this.TryFindMatch(bubble.Row, bubble.Column - 1, bubble.BubbleType);
        if (match != null)
            matches.Add(match);

        // Check right.
        match = this.TryFindMatch(bubble.Row, bubble.Column + 1, bubble.BubbleType);
        if (match != null)
            matches.Add(match);

        return matches;
    }
```

```
BubbleViewModel TryFindMatch(int row, int column, BubbleType bubbleType)
{
    return _allBubbles.SingleOrDefault(b =>
        b.Row == row &&
        b.Column == column &&
        b.BubbleType == bubbleType);
}
```

The SearchForGroup method uses a simple recursive algorithm to walk the bubble matrix. It adds each group member to the object's BubblesInGroup collection and then starts a new search with that bubble. When the search completes, the BubblesInGroup property of the BubbleGroup object can be used to process each bubble that was found. As we saw in the VerifyGroupMembership method previously, the Activate method is called on a BubbleGroup after the search completes. That method tells each bubble that it is in a bubble group:

```
internal void Activate()
{
    foreach (BubbleViewModel member in this.BubblesInGroup)
    {
        member.IsInBubbleGroup = true;
    }
}
```

The Deactivate method contains the same loop, only it sets IsInBubbleGroup to false on each bubble. DataTriggers in the View layer bind to that property in order to turn on/off visual effects for the bubble group under the cursor. You can see how that works by looking at the Style whose x:Key is 'BubbleGridStyle' in the BubbleViewResources.xaml file, if you're interested.

A ViewModel is a Model of a View

While creating ViewModel classes I often find the need to decide where to put certain pieces of code. The question often boils down to either putting it into the View's code-behind or the ViewModel. It can be tempting to put some code that logically belongs in a ViewModel object into a View, for the sake of convenience. I always regret doing it, and end up having to pull that code out of the code-behind at some point. As this chapter has shown, limiting your Views to only the code that is specific to their events, elements, resources, etc. enables you to keep the various application layers clear, logical, and loosely coupled. Separation of concerns is a worthwhile goal when writing software.

Chapter 5 – Animated Transitions

At this point we have gained a high-level perspective of the application's architecture. Armed with that knowledge we can now dive deep into how some challenging design problems were overcome. This chapter examines what happens after the user bursts a bubble group and the game state transition which accommodates that change.

What is an Animated Transition?

Software is all about state transitions. When a variable changes from one value to another, it has transitioned from one state to another. The simplest and most common state transitions occur sequentially and synchronously. For example, a method is invoked which transitions the state of one or more variables from one discrete value to another, and then returns the flow of execution back to the method that called it. All of that processing can occur in an inconceivably short amount of time, thanks to the power of modern computer hardware. This is the easiest and most natural way for software to operate.

That's all well and good, but there's a problem. We live in a physical world in which change gradually occurs. If you drop a ball it does not immediately appear on the ground. It has to fall first. Falling to the ground takes enough time that we are able to observe the ball during its state transition from "in hand" to "on ground." In other words, we can observe the ball passing through a series of intermediary altitudes between the ball's altitude in your hand and its altitude on the ground.

When you use a computer program it can be jarring and confusing when the objects on the screen do not behave similarly to what you would observe in an analogous situation in the physical world. Conversely, when objects on the screen emulate the physicality of the physical world it becomes easier to understand and more pleasurable to interact with the program. Therefore, in order to create software that people enjoy using it is sometimes necessary to animate transitions in the user interface.

This raises the question of, how?

Designing for Animated Transitions

The design problem of animating state transitions can be solved by drawing a clear boundary between logical state changes and visual state changes. This is yet another example of how MVVM can lead to good engineering practices. Logical state changes are managed by the ViewModel layer while the View layer is responsible for creating animated visual state changes. When visual state changes finish, the View informs the ViewModel to complete its state transition. This design keeps the View and ViewModel loosely coupled to each other, and does not reduce the testability of ViewModel classes. It also allows the View to decide how the visual animations should look and feel. A separation of concerns is established.

The implementation pattern I normally use is to have a ViewModel object raise an event that notifies the View when a state transition has begun. When the View handles that event it gets the destination value of the state transition from the ViewModel and uses that value to determine the To property of an animation. Once the animation is configured, the View runs it and waits for its Completed event to be raised. When the animation completes the visual state transition is done, at which point the View notifies the ViewModel that it is finished. Lastly, the ViewModel applies the destination value to the property that just underwent a transition.

That is the general idea. In BubbleBurst, however, things are a bit more complicated.

Animated Transitions in BubbleBurst

After the user bursts a group of bubbles many animated transitions occur. There are three transition phases, each of which begins after the previous phase completes. A phase can include multiple animated transitions that occur at the same time. A phase completes once all of its transitions are complete.

When a bubble group bursts, the first transition phase is responsible for fading away and removing all bubbles in the group.

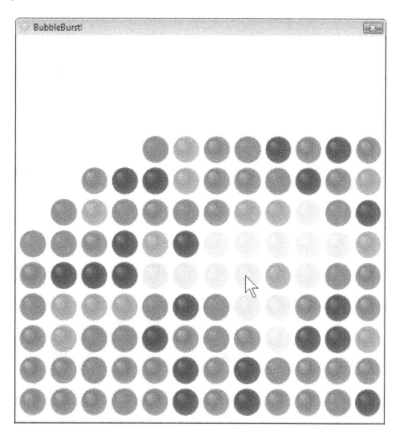

Once the bubble group has been removed, the next phase drops all bubbles that were above the group down into the vacated area. The screenshot below shows bubbles in the process of dropping down:

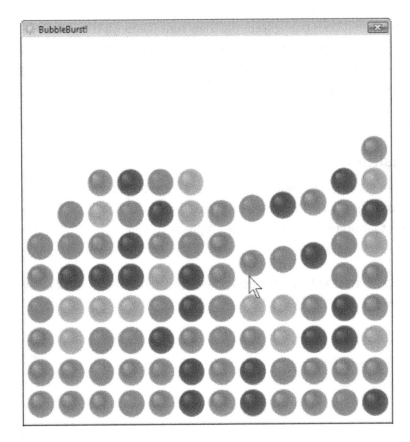

Once that phase completes, all bubbles move as far right as they can:

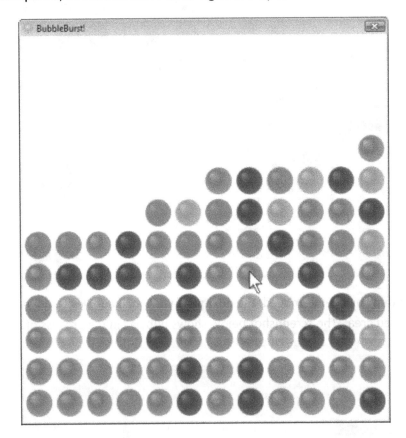

Creating Animated Transitions in the ViewModel

As explained earlier, the ViewModel and View are involved with orchestrating animated transitions. When the user clicks on a bubble it causes BubbleViewModel's BurstBubbleGroupCommand to execute. That command delegates to the BurstBubbleGroup method on the bubble matrix. When BubbleMatrixViewModel is told to burst the current bubble group, it ends up publishing a queue of BubblesTask objects to BubbleMatrixView. We will examine how the View processes those tasks in the next section of this chapter. For now, let's focus on how the ViewModel objects cooperate to create this queue of tasks. The following class diagram shows the key players involved:

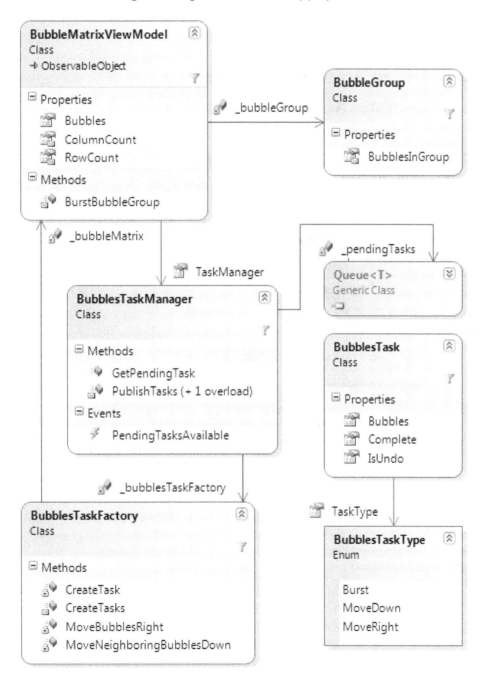

Our starting point is the BurstBubbleGroup method on BubbleMatrixViewModel. It utilizes the BubbleGroup class, which we saw in Chapter 4, to get a list of bubbles in the bubble group currently under the mouse cursor. If a bubble group is available, that list of bubbles is sent to BubblesTaskManager for further processing.

```
internal void BurstBubbleGroup()
{
    if (!this.IsIdle)
        throw new InvalidOperationException("...");

    var bubblesInGroup = _bubbleGroup.BubblesInGroup.ToArray();
    if (!bubblesInGroup.Any())
        return;

    _bubbleGroupSizeStack.Push(bubblesInGroup.Length);

    this.TaskManager.PublishTasks(bubblesInGroup);
}
```

The task manager is responsible for creating and publishing BubblesTask objects. Here is an abridged description of the BubblesTask class:

```
public class BubblesTask
{
    IEnumerable<BubbleViewModel> Bubbles { get; }
    Action Complete { get; }
    bool IsUndo { get; }
    BubblesTaskType TaskType { get; }
}
```

BubblesTaskManager uses a BubblesTaskFactory to create tasks. It places those tasks onto a queue, which is used later by the View's task processing routine. Here is the relevant code from BubblesTaskManager:

```
readonly BubblesTaskFactory _bubblesTaskFactory;
readonly Queue<BubblesTask> _pendingTasks;
readonly Stack<IEnumerable<BubblesTask>> _undoStack;

/// <summary>
/// Publishs a set of tasks that will burst a bubble group.
/// </summary>
internal void PublishTasks(BubbleViewModel[] bubblesInGroup)
{
    var tasks = _bubblesTaskFactory.CreateTasks(bubblesInGroup);
    this.ArchiveTasks(tasks);
    this.PublishTasks(tasks);
}

void ArchiveTasks(IEnumerable<BubblesTask> tasks)
{
    _undoStack.Push(tasks);
}
```

```
void PublishTasks(IEnumerable<BubblesTask> tasks)
{
    foreach (BubblesTask task in tasks)
    {
        _pendingTasks.Enqueue(task);
    }

    this.RaisePendingTasksAvailable();
}

void RaisePendingTasksAvailable()
{
    var handler = this.PendingTasksAvailable;
    if (handler != null)
    {
        handler(this, EventArgs.Empty);
    }
}
```

Don't worry about the _undoStack_ field for now. We will see how that fits into the picture in the next chapter. At this point we have seen the task management logic, but not how the BubblesTask objects are created. Let's turn our attention to BubblesTaskFactory to see how that works. The task manager calls CreateTasks on a task factory, which is where the tasks are created, as seen below:

```
/// <summary>
/// Creates a sequence of tasks that must be performed for the
/// specified collection of bubbles.
/// </summary>
/// <param name="bubblesInGroup">The bubbles for which tasks are created.</param>
internal IEnumerable<BubblesTask> CreateTasks(BubbleViewModel[] bubblesInGroup)
{
    var taskTypes = new BubblesTaskType[]
    {
        BubblesTaskType.Burst,
        BubblesTaskType.MoveDown,
        BubblesTaskType.MoveRight
    };

    // Dump the tasks into an array so that the query is not executed twice.
    return
        (from taskType in taskTypes
         select this.CreateTask(taskType, bubblesInGroup))
        .ToArray();
}
```

Here is where things start to get interesting! Each animated transition phase is represented by a value from the BubblesTaskType enumeration. An array of those values is created and used in a LINQ query that creates a BubblesTask for each phase. The CreateTask method is responsible for returning a BubblesTask instance that can be used to perform a certain type of task based on the list of bubbles in the group that was burst.

Here is the CreateTask method of BubblesTaskFactory:

```
BubblesTask CreateTask(BubblesTaskType taskType, BubbleViewModel[] bubblesInGroup)
{
    Func<IEnumerable<BubbleViewModel>> getBubbles;
    Action complete;
    switch (taskType)
    {
        case BubblesTaskType.Burst:
            getBubbles = delegate
            {
                _bubbleMatrix.IsIdle = false;
                return bubblesInGroup;
            };
            complete = delegate
            {
                foreach (BubbleViewModel bubble in bubblesInGroup)
                {
                    _bubbleMatrix.RemoveBubble(bubble);
                }
            };
            break;

        case BubblesTaskType.MoveDown:
            getBubbles = delegate
            {
                return this.MoveNeighboringBubblesDown(bubblesInGroup);
            };
            complete = delegate
            {
                /* Nothing to do here. */
            };
            break;

        case BubblesTaskType.MoveRight:
            getBubbles = delegate
            {
                return this.MoveBubblesRight();
            };
            complete = delegate
            {
                _bubbleMatrix.IsIdle = true;
                _bubbleMatrix.TryToEndGame();
            };
            break;

        default:
            throw new ArgumentException("...");
    }
    return new BubblesTask(taskType, false, getBubbles, complete);
}
```

When the 'Burst' task is being performed, the first thing it does is set the bubble matrix's IsIdle property to false. When the final phase completes it sets that property back to true. IsIdle is bound to by the BubbleMatrixView's IsEnabled property. The net effect of this property binding is that the UI will not respond to mouse clicks during an animated transition. The context menu will not open when the ViewModel is not idle because it, too, has its IsEnabled property bound to IsIdle. This ensures that the state of the bubble matrix is stable when a bubble group burst request is issued by the View, because the View cannot make a request during an animated transition.

Notice how BubblesTask's constructor is injected with two delegates: *getBubbles* and *complete*. Those delegates point to methods that execute when a task is about to be performed and immediately after it is finished, respectively. The *getBubbles* delegate is invoked by the View when it needs to create animations for the bubbles associated with a task. Determining that list of bubbles on demand enables BubblesTaskFactory's methods to analyze the state of the bubble matrix after the previous task(s) have already updated it. This allows the state transitions to be atomic. For example, the logic that moves bubbles down does not have to take into account which bubbles will be removed from the matrix by the previous task. They will already have been removed by the time that logic executes.

This method, from BubblesTaskFactory, shows how the logical state of the bubble matrix is updated so that bubbles move to the right. It returns a list of bubbles that it moved.

```
IEnumerable<BubbleViewModel> MoveBubblesRight()
{
    var movedBubbles = new List<BubbleViewModel>();
    for (int rowIndex = 0; rowIndex < _bubbleMatrix.RowCount; ++rowIndex)
    {
        var bubblesInRow =
            _bubbleMatrix.Bubbles.Where(b => b.Row == rowIndex).ToArray();
        // Skip empty rows and full rows.
        if (bubblesInRow.Length == 0 ||
            bubblesInRow.Length == _bubbleMatrix.ColumnCount)
            continue;

        for (int colIndex = _bubbleMatrix.ColumnCount - 1; colIndex > -1; --colIndex)
        {
            var bubble = bubblesInRow.SingleOrDefault(b => b.Column == colIndex);
            if (bubble != null)
            {
                // Find out how many cells between the bubble
                // and the last column have bubbles in them.
                int occupied =
                    bubblesInRow.Where(b => bubble.Column < b.Column).Count();

                // Now determine how many of the cells do not have a bubble in them.
                int empty = _bubbleMatrix.ColumnCount - 1 - bubble.Column - occupied;
                if (empty != 0)
                {
                    bubble.MoveTo(bubble.Row, bubble.Column + empty);
                    movedBubbles.Add(bubble);
                }
            }
        }
    }
    return movedBubbles;
}
```

The call to BubbleViewModel's MoveTo method does not result in a change to the location of a BubbleView element on the screen. It simply updates the bubble's internal representation of which cell in the bubble matrix it is currently in. It's up to the View to actually move the corresponding bubble visual to its new location.

Displaying Animated Transitions in the View

We have seen how the ViewModel layer creates and publishes a set of tasks that update the logical state of the application in response to bursting a bubble group. Now let's turn our attention to how BubbleMatrixView performs animated transitions on the bubbles it contains. The following class diagram shows the relevant objects and their members:

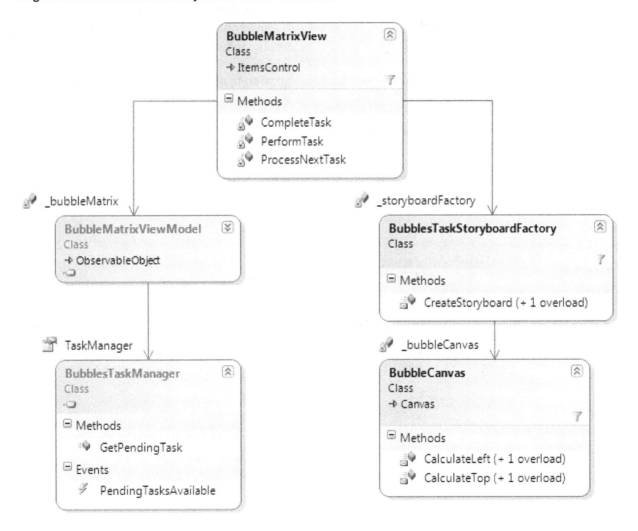

BubbleMatrixView subscribes to the PendingTasksAvailable event of the task manager. In the previous section we saw how that event is raised after the BubblesTaskFactory has created a list of tasks, which are placed onto a queue. Raising the event from the ViewModel lets the View know when to process those tasks and display animated transitions for the bubbles affected by the bubble group burst.

The following event handling method in BubbleMatrixView locates its ViewModel object and attaches a handler to the PendingTasksAvailable event:

```
void HandleDataContextChanged(object sender, DependencyPropertyChangedEventArgs e)
{
    _bubbleMatrix = base.DataContext as BubbleMatrixViewModel;

    if (_bubbleMatrix != null)
    {
        _bubbleMatrix.TaskManager.PendingTasksAvailable += delegate
        {
            this.ProcessNextTask();
        };
    }
}
```

When pending tasks are made available, three methods work together to process them and perform animated transitions. These methods are in the code-behind of BubbleMatrixView:

```
void ProcessNextTask()
{
    var task = _bubbleMatrix.TaskManager.GetPendingTask();
    if (task != null)
    {
        var storyboard = _storyboardFactory.CreateStoryboard(task);
        this.PerformTask(task, storyboard);
    }
}

void PerformTask(BubblesTask task, Storyboard storyboard)
{
    if (storyboard != null)
    {
        // There are some bubbles that need to be animated, so we must
        // wait until the Storyboard finishs before completing the task.
        storyboard.Completed += delegate { this.CompleteTask(task); };

        // Freeze the Storyboard to improve perf.
        storyboard.Freeze();

        // Start animating the bubbles associated with the task.
        storyboard.Begin(this);
    }
    else
    {
        // There are no bubbles associated with this task,
        // so immediately move to the task completion phase.
        this.CompleteTask(task);
    }
}

void CompleteTask(BubblesTask task)
{
    task.Complete();
```

```
    this.ProcessNextTask();
}
```

This simple mechanism is all that's required to process the task queue. The PerformTask method must check to see if its *storyboard* argument is null, because it is possible that a task could have no bubbles associated with it. This situation arises when, for example, there are no bubbles to move down after the user bursts a bubble group. When a task has no bubbles there is no need to run a Storyboard.

The task manager exposes a GetPendingTask method, which pops the next task off its queue and returns it. If the queue is empty, because all tasks have been processed, it returns null. The fact that a queue is used to store the tasks is unknown to the View. In this application it is not really necessary to encapsulate that detail, but in a larger system, especially one where Views are loaded as plug-ins, this level of encapsulation is an absolute requirement. ViewModel objects should not trust that Views will behave properly. ViewModels must take precautions against poorly written Views. Exceptions should be thrown when Views invoke ViewModel methods at the wrong time, or with invalid arguments. Collections of data should be exposed as read-only collections, such as ReadOnlyObservableCollection<T>, whenever possible.

What we have not yet seen is how the Storyboards that move BubbleViews are created. That is the responsibility of BubblesTaskStoryboardFactory.

The CreateStoryboard method called in the code above is shown here:

```
internal Storyboard CreateStoryboard(BubblesTask task)
{
    int millisecondsPerUnit;
    Func<ContentPresenter, double> getTo;
    DependencyProperty animatedProperty;
    IEnumerable<BubbleViewModel> bubbles;

    this.GetStoryboardCreationData(
        task,
        out millisecondsPerUnit,
        out getTo,
        out animatedProperty,
        out bubbles);

    return this.CreateStoryboard(
        task,
        millisecondsPerUnit,
        getTo,
        animatedProperty,
        bubbles.ToArray());
}
```

This method relies on two helper methods to get its job done. The first call is to GetStoryboardCreationData. That method determines the values that should be used to configure a Storyboard for the specified task type. It's a rather long method that does not provide much insight into how this logic works, so we won't bother reviewing it here. Instead, let's take a look at the logic that uses those configuration values to produce a Storyboard.

```
Storyboard CreateStoryboard(
    BubblesTask task,
    int millisecondsPerUnit,
    Func<ContentPresenter, double> getTo,
    DependencyProperty animatedProperty,
    BubbleViewModel[] bubbles)
{
    if (!bubbles.Any())
        return null;

    var storyboard = new Storyboard();
    var targetProperty = new PropertyPath(animatedProperty);
    var beginTime = TimeSpan.FromMilliseconds(0);
    var beginTimeIncrement =
        TimeSpan.FromMilliseconds(millisecondsPerUnit / bubbles.Count());

    foreach (ContentPresenter presenter in this.GetBubblePresenters(bubbles))
    {
        var bubble = presenter.DataContext as BubbleViewModel;
        var duration = CalculateDuration(task.TaskType, bubble, millisecondsPerUnit);
        var to = getTo(presenter);
        var anim = new EasingDoubleAnimation
        {
            BeginTime = beginTime,
            Duration = duration,
            Equation = EasingEquation.CubicEaseIn,
            To = to,
        };

        Storyboard.SetTarget(anim, presenter);
        Storyboard.SetTargetProperty(anim, targetProperty);

        if (IsTaskStaggered(task.TaskType))
        {
            beginTime = beginTime.Add(beginTimeIncrement);
        }

        storyboard.Children.Add(anim);
    }

    return storyboard;
}
```

The method seen above creates a Storyboard that contains an animation for every bubble associated with a BubblesTask. The type of animation created is EasingDoubleAnimation, which comes from my Thriple library on CodePlex. That animation uses Penner equations to determine its output values, which can be useful for creating elegant, natural movements in the user interface. Also note that each animation's BeginTime is set a successively longer duration, for the tasks that cause bubbles to move.

This helps create a more realistic feeling that the bubbles are falling like how objects fall in the physical world.

The duration of a bubble's animation is based on the distance it moves. Each cell in the bubble matrix represents a unit of space that requires a certain amount of time for the bubble to pass through. The CalculateDuration method takes care of figuring out how long each bubble should move for, as seen below:

```
static Duration CalculateDuration(
    BubblesTaskType taskType,
    BubbleViewModel bubble,
    int msPerUnit)
{
    int totalMs;
    switch (taskType)
    {
        case BubblesTaskType.Burst:
            totalMs = msPerUnit;
            break;
        case BubblesTaskType.MoveDown:
            totalMs = msPerUnit * Math.Abs(bubble.Row - bubble.PreviousRow);
            break;
        case BubblesTaskType.MoveRight:
            totalMs = msPerUnit * Math.Abs(bubble.Column - bubble.PreviousColumn);
            break;
    }
    return new Duration(TimeSpan.FromMilliseconds(totalMs));
}
```

There is more code involved with creating the Storyboards used to display animated transitions. I encourage you to explore that code in depth, but for the purposes of this chapter we have seen enough of it to understand how the View displays animated transitions.

Chapter 6 – Unlimited Undo with Animated Transitions

We all make mistakes. I make a lot of them, which is why BubbleBurst has support for unlimited undo.
You can un-burst a bubble group by clicking on the 'Undo' context menu item, or by pressing Ctrl + Z.
The application allows you to undo bursts all the way back to the initial state of the game, when the
bubble matrix is completely full of bubbles.   When you un-burst a bubble group the sequence of
animated transitions are run in reverse. This chapter reviews how I implemented that feature.

Responding to User Input

An undo operation is performed in response to user input, so the first step is to listen for the
appropriate input events. Since there are two ways to tell the game to perform an undo operation,
there are two code paths that lead to the undo functionality. BubbleBurstView listens for the Ctrl + Z
keystroke and calls Undo on BubbleMatrixViewModel.

```
void HandleMatrixDimensionsAvailable(object sender, EventArgs e)
{
    // Hook the keyboard event on the Window because this
    // control does not receive keystrokes.
    var window = Window.GetWindow(this);
    if (window != null)
    {
        window.PreviewKeyDown += this.HandleWindowPreviewKeyDown;
    }
    this.StartNewGame();
}

void HandleWindowPreviewKeyDown(object sender, KeyEventArgs e)
{
    bool undo =
        Keyboard.Modifiers == ModifierKeys.Control &&
        e.Key == Key.Z;

    if (undo && _bubbleBurst.CanUndo)
    {
        _bubbleBurst.BubbleMatrix.Undo();
        e.Handled = true;
    }
}
```

When the user clicks on the 'Undo' context menu item it causes BubbleBurstViewModel's
UndoCommand to execute.

```
public ICommand UndoCommand
{
    get { return new RelayCommand(this.BubbleMatrix.Undo, () => this.CanUndo); }
}

public bool CanUndo
{
    get { return this.GameOver == null && this.BubbleMatrix.CanUndo; }
```

```
}
```

The real work of performing an undo operation is handled by objects deeper down in the object graph.

Creating Undo Tasks

BubbleMatrixViewModel exposes an Undo method that is invoked by the code seen in the previous section. That method merely delegates the work off to the task manager, because undoing a bubble group burst involves reusing the tasks that performed the burst.

```
/// <summary>
/// Reverts the game state to how it was before
/// the most recent group of bubbles was burst.
/// </summary>
public void Undo()
{
    if (this.CanUndo)
    {
        // Throw away the last bubble group size,
        // since that burst is about to be undone.
        _bubbleGroupSizeStack.Pop();

        this.TaskManager.Undo();
    }
}

internal bool CanUndo
{
    get { return this.IsIdle && this.TaskManager.CanUndo; }
}
```

As you can see in the following code snippet from BubblesTaskManager, the code involved with undoing a bubble group burst looks quite similar to the code required to perform the burst in the first place.

```
/// <summary>
/// Publishs a set of tasks that will undo the previous bubble burst.
/// </summary>
internal void Undo()
{
    var originalTasks = _undoStack.Pop();
    var undoTasks = _bubblesTaskFactory.CreateUndoTasks(originalTasks);
    this.PublishTasks(undoTasks);
}
```

The _undoStack has collections of tasks pushed onto it when the user bursts bubble groups by the PublishTasks method seen in the previous chapter. In the Undo method those collections of tasks are popped from the stack to create new tasks. Instead of calling the task factory's CreateTasks method, when performing an undo operation the CreateUndoTasks method is called. That method's parameter is the list of tasks created by a previous invocation of the CreateTasks method. Each of those tasks provides the information needed to create a new set of "undo tasks" that return the game state to how it was before the original tasks were performed.

Here is the CreateUndoTasks logic from BubblesTaskFactory:

```
internal IEnumerable<BubblesTask> CreateUndoTasks(IEnumerable<BubblesTask> tasks)
{
    return
        (from task in tasks.Reverse()
         select this.CreateUndoTask(task))
        .ToArray();
}

BubblesTask CreateUndoTask(BubblesTask originalTask)
{
    var bubbles = originalTask.Bubbles.ToList();
    Func<IEnumerable<BubbleViewModel>> getBubbles;
    Action complete;
    switch (originalTask.TaskType)
    {
        case BubblesTaskType.MoveRight:
            getBubbles = delegate
            {
                _bubbleMatrix.IsIdle = false;
                bubbles.ForEach(b => b.BeginUndo());
                return bubbles;
            };
            complete = delegate
            {
                bubbles.ForEach(b => b.EndUndo());
            };
            break;
        case BubblesTaskType.MoveDown:
            getBubbles = delegate
            {
                bubbles.ForEach(b => b.BeginUndo());
                return bubbles;
            };
            complete = delegate
            {
                bubbles.ForEach(b => b.EndUndo());
            };
            break;
        case BubblesTaskType.Burst:
            getBubbles = delegate
            {
                bubbles.ForEach(b => _bubbleMatrix.AddBubble(b));
                return bubbles;
            };
            complete = delegate
            {
                _bubbleMatrix.IsIdle = true;
            };
            break;
        default:
            throw new ArgumentException("...");
    }
    return new BubblesTask(originalTask.TaskType, true, getBubbles, complete);
```

}

Each BubblesTask returned by that method has its IsUndo property set to true, via the second constructor parameter. That property is inspected by the View's BubblesTaskStoryboardFactory when it is deciding how to animate the bubbles to their new locations. When the user bursts a bubble group, the bottommost bubbles fall first and the rightmost bubbles move to the right first. The opposite is true for when the user performs an undo operation.

Another point of interest in the method seen above is how the first two tasks call the BeginUndo and EndUndo methods on each bubble whose location is affected. Those method calls ensure that the bubbles return the proper values from their PreviousRow and PreviousColumn properties. This is necessary for creating accurate Duration and To values for the animations used to move the bubbles to their new locations. Before we dive into that, first let's review how bubble locations are managed.

Managing Bubble Locations

In order for a bubble to know where to move to when the user performs an undo operation, each of its locations in the bubble matrix is archived. BubbleViewModel makes use of a helper class called BubbleLocationManager to store its location history.

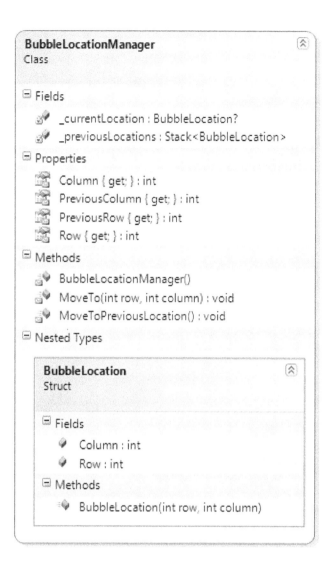

BubbleLocationManager is informed whenever its owning bubble is told to move to a new location in the bubble matrix. When an undo operation is performed, the MoveToPreviousLocation method is called, which results in a BubbleLocation being popped from the _previousLocations stack and used as the new current location.

BubbleViewModel makes use of its location manager via delegation from its Row, Column, PreviousRow, and PreviousColumn properties. The one exception to this is when the BeginUndo method is called on a bubble, which we saw in the previous section. Between the calls to BeginUndo and EndUndo a bubble ignores its location manager, which has no concept of being involved with an undo operation. That logic from BubbleViewModel is seen below:

```
readonly BubbleLocationManager _locationManager;
int? _prevColumnDuringUndo, _prevRowDuringUndo;

internal void BeginUndo()
{
    _prevRowDuringUndo = this.Row;
    _prevColumnDuringUndo = this.Column;
```

```
        _locationManager.MoveToPreviousLocation();
}

internal void EndUndo()
{
    // Now that the Undo operation is finished,
    // it's back to business as usual.
    _prevRowDuringUndo = null;
    _prevColumnDuringUndo = null;
}

public int PreviousColumn
{
    get
    {
        if (_prevColumnDuringUndo.HasValue)
            return _prevColumnDuringUndo.Value;
        else
            return _locationManager.PreviousColumn;
    }
}

public int PreviousRow
{
    get
    {
        if (_prevRowDuringUndo.HasValue)
            return _prevRowDuringUndo.Value;
        else
            return _locationManager.PreviousRow;
    }
}
```

This is an implementation detail peculiar to the BubbleBurst game. The general concept, however, of keeping a helper class simple by not polluting it with logic for unrelated features, like unlimited undo, is relevant in many situations. It helps minimize the impacts of such features on the code base.

Benefits of a Task-based Architecture

Both this chapter and the previous one focused on features of BubbleBurst that leverage a task-based architecture. Another name for this type of design pattern is Unit of Work. By having the ViewModel create objects that represent a task to be performed by the View, and associating each task with a list of objects to manipulate, the application gained animated transitions and unlimited undo functionality. Implementing the symmetry between bursting and un-bursting a group of bubbles was simply a matter of applying and reverting effects of three tasks. This is a powerful and flexible approach to creating loosely coupled layers in any application.

Chapter 7 – The Game-Over Dialog

Once there are no bubble groups left for the user to burst the game is over. When the game ends a modal dialog is shown, asking the user if a new game should start or if the application should close. The user cannot click on any bubbles or undo the previous burst at this point. The game-over dialog is shown below:

When the game-over dialog appears on the screen it bounces into place. If the user clicks on 'PLAY AGAIN', the dialog flies into the background while a new set of bubbles fills the window. I refer to the initial bounce-into-view animation as the "intro", and the fly-into-background animation as the "outro." The intro animation begins when the GameOverView's Visibility is set to Visible, and the outro animation begins in response to some code that executes when the user clicks the 'PLAY AGAIN' Hyperlink control.

Opening the GameOver Dialog

GameOverView is a user control that resides in the top-level View, called BubbleBurstView. It is not shown in a separate window, like a normal dialog box. Since it is a child element of BubbleBurstView, it must be collapsed while the user is playing a game. Once the game comes to an end, the GameOverView's Visibility property is set to Visible.

An abridged version of BubbleBurstView's XAML structure looks like this:

```
<UserControl xmlns:view="clr-namespace:BubbleBurst.View">
  <UserControl.ContextMenu>
    <ContextMenu>
      <MenuItem Header="Undo" />
      <MenuItem Header="Restart" />
    </ContextMenu>
  </UserControl.ContextMenu>
  <Grid>
    <view:BubbleMatrixView />
    <view:GameOverView />
  </Grid>
</UserControl>
```

Notice that the GameOverView is declared after/below the BubbleMatrixView. This ensures that it will render on top of the BubbleMatrixView, with respect to Z-order. Now let's take a closer look at how the visibility of GameOverView is controlled. The following XAML, from BubbleBurstView, is responsible for showing and hiding the game-over dialog:

```
<view:GameOverView DataContext="{Binding Path=GameOver}">
  <view:GameOverView.Style>
    <Style TargetType="{x:Type view:GameOverView}">
      <Style.Triggers>
        <DataTrigger Binding="{Binding Path=.}" Value="{x:Null}">
          <Setter Property="Visibility" Value="Collapsed" />
        </DataTrigger>
      </Style.Triggers>
    </Style>
  </view:GameOverView.Style>
</view:GameOverView>
```

The basic idea is to use a DataTrigger to collapse the View when its DataContext is null. Its DataContext is bound to the GameOver property of the BubbleBurstViewModel, which is assigned an instance of GameOverViewModel when a game ends. That property is set to null when a new game begins. Here is the code from BubbleBurstViewModel that manages the lifetime of GameOverViewModel objects:

```
public BubbleBurstViewModel()
{
    this.BubbleMatrix = new BubbleMatrixViewModel();

    this.BubbleMatrix.GameEnded += delegate
    {
        this.GameOver = new GameOverViewModel(this.BubbleMatrix);
        this.GameOver.RequestClose += this.HandleGameOverRequestClose;
    };
}

void HandleGameOverRequestClose(object sender, EventArgs e)
{
    this.GameOver.RequestClose -= this.HandleGameOverRequestClose;
    this.GameOver = null;
}
```

```
public GameOverViewModel GameOver
{
    get { return _gameOver; }
    private set
    {
        if (value == _gameOver)
            return;

        _gameOver = value;

        base.RaisePropertyChanged("GameOver");
    }
}
```

Once again we see how a ViewModel maintains the logical state of a user interface, while the Views bind against it to present that state in a visual manner.

Closing the GameOver Dialog

When the user clicks on the 'PLAY AGAIN' link it causes some code to execute in the GameOverView code-behind. That event handling method tells the bubble matrix to start a new game and begins a Storyboard which causes the game-over dialog to fly away. Having a new set of bubbles emerge while the game-over dialog disappears into the background provides an exciting aspect to the experience of starting a new game. The code that orchestrates the outro animation is seen below:

```
public GameOverView()
{
    InitializeComponent();

    _outroStoryboard = _contentBorder.Resources["OutroStoryboard"] as Storyboard;

    base.DataContextChanged += this.HandleDataContextChanged;
}

void HandleDataContextChanged(object sender, DependencyPropertyChangedEventArgs e)
{
    _gameOver = base.DataContext as GameOverViewModel;
}

void HandlePlayAgainHyperlinkClick(object sender, RoutedEventArgs e)
{
    _gameOver.StartNewGame();
    _outroStoryboard.Begin(this);
}

void HandleOutroCompleted(object sender, EventArgs e)
{
    _gameOver.Close();
}
```

The last piece of the puzzle is how GameOverViewModel's Close method works. When the outro animation finishes that method is invoked, causing GameOverView to disappear. The

GameOverViewModel notifies BubbleBurstViewModel that it wants to close by raising its RequestClose event.

```
/// <summary>
/// Closes the game-over dialog.
/// </summary>
public void Close()
{
    this.RaiseRequestClose();
}

void RaiseRequestClose()
{
    var handler = this.RequestClose;
    if (handler != null)
    {
        handler(this, EventArgs.Empty);
    }
}
```

As we saw in the previous section, when that event is raised BubbleBurstViewModel sets its GameOver property to null. That property change causes the DataTrigger in BubbleBurstView to set the dialog's Visibility property to 'Collapsed.' At that point the user can start playing another game of BubbleBurst.

Chapter 8 – Recap

Throughout this e-book we have covered many topics and explored several techniques for overcoming challenging design problems in an MVVM architecture. Let's take a moment to review everything that we covered.

Recap

Our journey started with a quick overview of the BubbleBurst application, how to play it, and where to find the source code. Following that there was a refresher on WPF and MVVM, as they are used in BubbleBurst.

We took a tour of the View layer, and examined how the Views fit together to provide a compelling user interface. Afterwards we visited the ViewModel layer and saw how the logical state of the user interface is treated as a first-class citizen of the application. At several points we stopped to reflect on how one can create a separation of concerns by using good judgment and common sense to decide if code should live in the ViewModel or in a View's code-behind file.

Once we had a high-level understanding of the application architecture the real fun began. We saw how animated transitions can improve the user experience, and took a deep dive into how they work in BubbleBurst. Next we saw how the task-based pattern used for providing animated transitions was naturally extended to allow the user to perform unlimited undo operations that also result in animated transitions.

We wrapped up with a tour of the game-over dialog. We saw how it is opened and closed by a DataTrigger. We also reviewed small snippets of event handling code in the GameOverView that allowed the dialog to be animated away while a new game started filling the window with bubbles.

At no point did we see any ViewModel objects referencing UI elements. The BubbleBurst user interface could be replaced with a whole new set of Views and no changes would be necessary in the ViewModel layer (unless those new Views required functionality not currently available). MVVM makes life better!

Special Thanks

There are many people that I would like to thank for their input on this project.

First and foremost, I would like to thank **Johann Sebastian Bach**, **George Frideric Handel**, **Franz Schubert**, **Felix Mendelssohn**, and **Steve Reich**. Their music provided me with the inspiration needed to push my limits and expand my horizons, with regards to the technical, artistic, and literary aspects of the project. I would also like to thank all of the musicians I listened to who performed the music with such passion and elegance.

If it wasn't for the invaluable visual design and user experience suggestions by **Nathan Dunlap** and **Stuart Mayhew**, two of my colleagues at IdentityMine [http://identitymine.com], the BubbleBurst game would not be nearly as attractive and usable as it is. I also appreciate the visual design input that my friend **Grant Hinkson** gave me, which helped me add an extra bit of polish to the UI. I take full responsibility for any blemishes in the BubbleBurst user interface.

Another person who deserves credit is **Andrew Whiddett**, CTO of IdentityMine. He gave me an insightful code review and suggested some brilliant ideas for improving the architecture. The application's use of a task-based mediation system fell out of our conversations.

Special thanks also go to **Karl Shifflett** for reviewing the manuscript and giving great feedback. He kindly set aside time to read and comment on this document, even though he was in the middle of working on his own projects.

Last, but certainly not least, I would like to thank my lovely girlfriend **Sarah**. This e-book was her idea. She gave me several great suggestions for improving the application's visual design, and lots of encouragement along the way. Sarah kindly and patiently tolerated me spending all of Valentine's Day weekend in my apartment writing these words.

www.ingramcontent.com/pod-product-compliance
Lightning Source LLC
Chambersburg PA
CBHW060507060326
40689CB00020B/4667